# Activate Your Yes

## A Breakthrough Guide to Obey God and Stop Overthinking Your Way Out of It

Kim Hardy

Published in the United States of America.

For permission requests, please contact: Kim Hardy kim@kimhardy.org

Book Design by Monica Hardy



ISBN: 9798290812687

Library of Congress Control Number:

Printed in the United States of America

To Dexter — my steady place, my partner in every yes. Thank you for walking with me through every season.

To Danielle, Philip, Monica, Jasmine, and Hope — Keep saying yes–even when it's hard, even when no one sees. Never forget: Your yes has Kingdom impact that will last beyond you.

**But be doers of the word, and not hearers only, deceivingyourselves.**

**–James 1:22**

# Contents

# INTRODUCTION

## THIS IS YOUR MOMENT

You probably know God has a Kingdom assignment on your life. And I want you to know it's completely understandable if you're still trying to process what that really means. Maybe it's just starting to take shape.

Or maybe you're like me.

You've already said yes to your current assignment. You're showing up the best you know how. Even then, it helps to be reminded that your obedience must be activated daily. On the days when it feels small or slow, God is still working things out.

Or maybe you've known for a while what your assignment is, but you keep procrastinating, overthinking, and allowing doubt to keep you from fully stepping into it. You might even wonder if it's too late, or you're too old, tired, or behind to start a new assignment.But here's what I want you to know: it's not too late. And you're not too far gone.

If you continue to sense God nudging and prompting you to do something, it's time to move. Whatever it is, you need to be encouraged to obey God. I pray that this book will serve as your invitation and challenge to trust God and step fully into obedience, even when it feels costly.

Activating Your Yes is not about striving harder. It's about surrendering to God faster and putting your obedience into motion. Because every time you say yes, you join God in advancing His Kingdom through your life.

## THE TENSION YOU FEEL IS REAL

There is always a tension between where you are and where your soul knows you're meant to be.

You can sense it. We all can. Wherever you are right now, deep down your soul knows that God wants to do more for you and through you.

You were created for more than autopilot living. More than waking up tired, rushing through your morning routine, sitting in meetings that drain you, paying bills, planning a vacation once or twice a year, and serving in church, like that's your only assignment.

That's not your whole story. And that's definitely not the only thing God had in mind when He formed you. You weren't just made to exist. The best pages haven't even been lived yet.

You were created to walk with God, hear His voice, and make the Kingdom impact that He designed for your life before time began. God's assignment for your life was set in motion long before you ever said yes.

> "For we are His workmanship, created in Christ Jesus for good works, which God prepared beforehand, that we should walk in them." (Ephesians 2:10)

## Spirit-Empowered Faith

Let me pause and say something I wish I had embraced years ago: You can't fulfill a God-given assignment withoutGod-given faith. Faith isn't about forcing something to happen. It's not manufactured—it's received. You can't fulfill a God-sized assignment with man-made strength.

You can't muster the kind of faith it takes to walk out your purpose. That kind of faith doesn't come from willpower.It comes from God's power. It's not self-generated. It's Spirit-empowered.

Looking to Jesus, the founder and perfecter of our faith. (Hebrews 12:2)

Jesus starts your faith, strengthens it, and completes it. He is both the Author and the Finisher.

## Walk in What's Been Prepared

Ephesians 2:10 reminds us that you were "created in Christ Jesus for good works, which God prepared beforehand , that we should walk in them.

It means you weren't saved just to goto heaven. You were saved to partner with God as He brings His Kingdom—His rule and reign—into the world through your life.

Not just on Sundays. Not just when you feel strong. But every day, in the ordinary places where faith feels costly and obedience feels small.

The Kingdom of God is where things align with God's heart. It's where His will is done, on earth as it is in heaven. And whenever you forgive, choose integrity, speak life, make disciples, share the gospel, show up with love and compassion, or respond to His nudge instead of your fear, you walk in what He prepared for you.

That's Kingdom.

God's Kingdom doesn't advance through perfection. It advances through obedience. So don't overlook the moments that seem minor. Those are the places where God touches the earth through you. And as you keep moving, something powerful happens. God starts to reveal more. You start to hear Him more clearly. The dots begin to connect. And what once felt vague becomes clear.

This is how your assignment unfolds. Not in one giant leap, but through daily surrender. This is how God's Kingdom, His rule, and His reign keep showing up in the world through people who say yes with action.

## ACTIVATE YOUR YES

So, before you start wondering how you'll accomplish the call on your life, ask yourself:

- What has God already placed in front of me?
- Where do I feel the Spirit nudging me again and again?
- What have I been delaying that might actually be my next step?

You don't have to overthink it. But you do have to be surrendered, Spirit-led and walk it out. You do have to participate. Because the more you walk with God, and the more you obey, the more you'll see He's been working all along.

## WHEN OBEDIENCE IS THE ASSIGNMENT

Writing this book is part of my assignment from God. If we were sitting across from each other right now, I'd gently ask you this question: "What's your next step?" Because here's the truth: you don't need another sign. You don't need to have it all figured out. You need to move with what God has already placed before you. One step is enough when it's led by Him.

And if you've already said yes, let this be your reminder–obedience doesn't end with one moment. It continues in the unseen, the repeated, and the surrendered. Staying faithful is part of the assignment. God keeps working through every step you take. And honestly, every yes responds to the God who loves you immensely and immeasurably. As you live out your assignment, remember this isn't just about doing something for God; it's about becoming someone with Him. Every step of obedience forms you, and that formation is the real movement.

## NEVER FORGET: YOUR YES IS TIME-SENSITIVE

You and I aren't here forever. That truth isn't meant to scare you. It's meant to wake something up inside of both of us. There is a yes in you—a living, breathing Kingdom yes that needs to be released every day. Psalm 90:12 says, "So teach us to number our days that we may get a heart of wisdom." Time is a gift, and wisdom is knowing how to use it.

Now, take a deep breath. And let this be the moment you say yes and walk it out. Only you can do it. So, what will you choose? Will you wait? Will you wonder? Or will you move with God–right here, right now?

# Chapter 1

# YOUR YES TO GOD IS AT A CROSSROADS

**I DIDN'T LOOK LIKE SOMEONE WHO WAS FALLING APART.**

I was leading Bible studies, serving faithfully, and singing loud during worship. From the outside, I looked like a woman deeply rooted in faith. I was checking all the boxes.

But inside? I was a high-functioning depressed pastor's wife.

I was doing all the things that should have signaled obedience. I was serving, showing up, and leading. But the truth is, I had started living with a yes that only reached as far as my comfort zone.

That may feel like a lot to unpack up front. But let me warn you now, in this book there is no tiptoeing around the hard stuff, no waiting for the perfect moment or the perfect feeling.I promise, I'll share more of my story soon. For now, I want you to lean in and understand:

> **Your yes to God is not a one-time decision. It's a daily invitation to trust and obey at every crossroads life brings.**

And for me, that truth became real when God allowed me to run out of strength so I could run into His arms. He didn't just restore me; He redeemed my whole life and story. He taught me how to trust and obey. He called out the yes hidden in me, not to shame me, but to wake me to His presence, power, and plan.

That awakening changed everything. What began as a season of total breakdown became the starting point of a supernatural breakthrough. And I haven't stopped telling the story. Thankfully, God was too faithful to let me settle beneath what He had destined for me.

## THE CHOICE IS YOURS

Every follower of Jesus eventually arrives at the intersection of comfort and calling. It's the place where we wrestle with this question:

**Will I choose the path of obedience, even if it costs me?**

This struggle between what's familiar and what's faithful isn't new. God's people have always been called to choose. Think about Joshua's words to Israel: "Choose this day whom you will serve." (Joshua 24:15)

Not just once, but again and again. Why? Because the human heart drifts. Because obedience requires recalibration. This chapter is an opportunity to do that.

So before you read on, pause.

Take a breath.

Now ask yourself, not from pressure but from curiosity:

What has the Holy Spirit been speaking to me?

Where have I been hesitating?

Where is comfort keeping me from calling?

Look beyond the stories you've rehearsed and the doubts that seem reasonable. And instead, pay attention to the places where you feel that quiet tug—the one that both stirs and unsettles you.That could be the very place where God is inviting you into a deeper yes.

We all have those moments. The ones where we have to choose: obedience or comfort. Obedience or convenience. Obedience or routine. Obedience or you fill in the blank. I know this is much easier said than done. Activating Your Yes is a very intentional decision.

Activating Your Yes means recognizing that the things that keep you comfortable may be the very things God is asking you to surrender.

## YOU DON'T DRIFT INTO OBEDIENCE

If most Christians were asked whether they want to live with bold obedience, the answer would be yes. So why is it that we sometimes live a life in total opposition to that desire?

It's because obedience is not just something we should desire. It's something we have to deliberately choose, day after day. It's not a byproduct of comfort or convenience. Obedience can be costly, but always significant. You step into it with intention, conviction, and a willingness to follow, even when it costs you something.

Paul writes in Galatians 5:25, "If we live by the Spirit, let us also keep in step with the Spirit." This means obedience is less about what you feel and more about what you *do*. It's the daily act of following God's lead, even when the path isn't clear.

Every decision you make is either an expression of your yes or a quiet surrender to a no. You're either living from surrender or resistance. You're either yielding to the Spirit or yielding to self-preservation and disobedience. There is no neutral ground.

We often wait for God to make it unmistakably safe before we move. More often than not, God waits for us to move before He makes it clear. He doesn't part the waters until we step in. It won't always feel dramatic or easy, yet when you choose obedience, you open the door for God to work.

So, ask Him.

Where do I need to give You my Yes?

## Chapter 2

# GOD ISN'T ASKING FOR A PERFECT YES

**He's asking for an activated yes.** One that costs something. One that changes your schedule. One that makes you uncomfortable. And one that stretches your faith until it stops being theory and starts becoming testimony.

You don't need more information. You don't need another conference or small group meeting. You need to trust the God who called you, activated something in you, and now empowers your Yes through Him. This isn't about trying harder or doing more. It's about learning to move in partnership with the One who already placed His Spirit inside of you.

> "For it is God who works in you, both to will and to work for his good pleasure" (Philippians 2:13).

God's not just giving you the desire—He's giving you the power. That's how you begin to Activate Your Yes: not in your strength, but by learning to respond to His prompting with trust, obedience, and motion.

## HALF OBEDIENCE

Even when you're already walking in your assignment, there's always the subtle danger of falling into the trap of saying, "I'll do it later." Later, when it feels safer. Later, when I have more money. Later, when I have more time. Later, when I'm less afraid of what obedience might cost. But delayed obedience can still rob you of the impact God wants to release through you now.

> But here's what I've learned the hard way: Later becomes a dangerous way to live when time is limited and faith is required. Living a half-obedient yes is still disobedience.

It chips away at your joy, your peace, and your quality of life. Nothing robs your soul faster than knowing you're called to more but settling for less. Disobedience doesn't always announce itself. It shows up as inner restlessness, quiet frustration, and holy discontent. When God places a "more" in your spirit and you choose "less," it creates spiritual friction. This isn't about condemnation. It's a divine invitation. That deep sense that you're meant for something greater is a gift from God. Ignoring it isn't passive. It is a subtle act of disobedience that can leave your soul parched. It's the weight of an unfulfilled assignment, a burden God never intended for you to carry.

It can look like:

- **A dullness in your spirit:** The laughter doesn't come as easily. You might find yourself going through the motions, smiling on the outside, but feeling flat or empty on the inside. The vibrant colors of life seem a little muted.

- **A constant hum of anxiety:** True peace feels elusive. Your mind might race even when you're trying to rest, replaying conversations or worrying about the future. You feel unsettled, unable to truly relax and trust.

- **A diminishing quality of life:** Relationships might feel strained or superficial because you're less present. Your work, even if it's "good," lacks genuine fulfillment. You're simply existing, rather than truly living with passion and purpose.

This subtle erosion happens because when God calls you to more, He's inviting you into a deeper alignment with His design for you. When you resist or delay that Yes, even subtly, you are creating a spiritual tension. It's like trying to force a square peg into a round hole; it doesn't fit, and the friction causes wear and tear on your soul. That very restlessness is not a sign of your failure, but proof that your Yes is still alive, still yearning to be activated. It's God's relentless love, gently but persistently nudging you back to the path of freedom and abundant life.

## MY YES LOOKED GOOD ON THE OUTSIDE

For a long time, I thought I understood what it meant to live by faith. But when I looked at the actual rhythms of my life—the way I thought, the way I lived, the way I dealt with fear, the way I delayed obedience and hid behind prayer and busyness—unfortunately, my faith looked more like maintenance than movement.

And that brings us to rhythms. Because your life isn't just a series of isolated moments; it's an accumulation of habits, choices, and patterns that, over time, either lead you closer to God's activated plan or subtly pull you away. See, unhealthy rhythms are often quiet. They are the silent architects of that "chipping away" I mentioned earlier.

You can be doing "good" things while still avoiding obedience. You're busy but empty. Connected but unseen. Moving, but stuck. They are the unspoken agreements you make with distraction, with procrastination, with fear, or with the comfort of the familiar. These rhythms, though seemingly small, can become spiritual ruts, making you feel stuck even when you're moving.

Below is a great starting place to reflect and assess where you are in your rhythms:

- **Consider the rhythm of your thoughts:** Are they constantly spiraling into worry, or are you intentionally redirecting them to truth?
- **Think about the rhythm of your responses:** Do you react out of old patterns of fear or anger, or do you pause to seek God's wisdom?
- **Examine the rhythm of your time:** Is it filled with busyness that drains you, or with intentional moments that replenish your spirit and align you with your calling?

These rhythms, whether conscious or unconscious, are shaping your spiritual landscape. They determine whether your yes remains dormant, a quiet aspiration, or whether it becomes activated.

The good news is that you have the power to choose your rhythms. Good rhythms help you on the journey to Activate Your Yes and an obedient life because they create the spiritual conditions for God's power to flow freely. They are the consistent, intentional choices that align your daily walk with your divine calling. When you commit to rhythms of presence, of truth, of surrender, and of courageous action, you begin to experience a life of profound movement. A life where your yes is not just a word, but a powerful, unstoppable force for God's glory.

Before we dive more into rhythms, we need to confront the silent no that may be running the show.

## SOUL CHECK-INS

These questions are designed to invite you into a deeper, more honest conversation with yourself and with God. You don't have to answer them all. Just begin with one or two that resonate most with you. Let the Holy Spirit reveal truth to your heart. Consider journaling your responses or discussing them with a trusted spiritual mentor.

1. What's one place in your life where you sense God is gently drawing you closer—even if you're not sure what comes next?
2. What does your next "yes" make possible—not just for you, but for the people connected to your assignment?
3. What would change if you believed that God isn't disappointed in you, but actually delighted to walk with you—right here, right now?
4. Where in your story do you feel both afraid and alive—and could that be the place God is inviting your next step?

Chapter 3

# IT'S TIME TO CONFRONT YOUR "NO"

**A few weeks ago, our microwave stopped working.** The one above the stove we'd used every day for eight years just completely went kaput. There were no more dings, no more heat, I mean NOTHING. It quit on us without notice. So, we did what any practical person would do—we pulled the spare microwave out of the garage and set it up on the counter just a few feet away.

Problem solved, right?

Except it wasn't. Because for weeks—not days—without thinking, we kept walking back to the broken one. We'd open it, put our plate in, only to realize again: this stupid thing does not work.

The crazy part is we knew it didn't work. We experienced the brokenness of that microwave day in and day out. And although we knew there was a perfectly fine microwave working on the other counter, we kept going back.

Our habits and patterns were trained to go to the old one above the stove.

We weren't trying to return to the broken microwave. But we didn't realize that for eight years, we had conditioned and trained ourselves to follow a familiar pattern. That autopilot was embedded in our minds, and even though it no longer worked, we kept going back.

It wasn't logical, it was a habit. Familiarity. Comfort. My way of doing life.

And this is where it gets real in our spiritual lives: unless you spiritually and strategically disrupt your disobedient patterns, your body and mind will keep going back. Even when the Spirit wants you to move forward.

The truth is, we don't always act on the truth. We act on what's familiar.

## THE BRAIN IS WIRED FOR FAMILIARITY, NOT TRANSFORMATION

As I write this book to help you (and me) activate our Yes, we can't skip over how the brain works.

Here's the fact: your brain loves familiarity.

It's wired for efficiency, not transformation. That's why you keep reaching for the same broken "microwave" in your life, even after you know it doesn't work. Your nervous system is trained by repetition. What you do consistently, even if it's dysfunctional, feels safer than what's unknown.

Psychiatrist and author Dr. Curt Thompson, who writes extensively on the intersection of faith, neuroscience, and spiritual formation, explains it this way:

> "We all live at the mercy of the stories we tell ourselves."

Most of those stories are stored deep in your neural wiring, operating on autopilot. So, unless you interrupt the pattern, you'll unconsciously keep saying no to God... while thinking you're saying yes.

But the good news? God designed the brain to change.

It's called neuroplasticity.

Neuroplasticity is the brain's ability to rewire and form new connections. Just because you've lived a certain way doesn't mean you must keep living that way.

Romans 12:2 says, "Do not be conformed to this world, but be transformed by the renewal of your mind...". The Greek word for "transformed" is (metamorphoō), a complete change, like a caterpillar becoming a butterfly. That transformation isn't just spiritual; it's neurological. The word for "renewal" (anakainōsis) means a full renovation, not a tweak.

That means your mind must be reshaped by truth, not just intention. That takes practice. It takes yielding, repentance, and persistence.It takes what Ephesians 4:22-24 calls "putting off the old self" and "putting on the new."

## OBEDIENCE REQUIRES REWIRING

Let me say it plainly.

If you've been struggling to obey God—even though you want to—it may not be just because you're disobedient. It may be because an internal no has trained you for years.

Here's the hope: as you align with God's truth and walk in the Spirit, your brain starts to build new pathways, pathways of faith, surrender, and trust.

That means when you choose obedience, even when it's uncomfortable, you're literally rewiring your brain to walk in step with the Spirit.

Every activated Yes retrains your inner world.

## YOUR "NO" IS ALSO AN INVITATION

It's an invitation to slow down. To pay attention. To ask:

- What have I been reaching for that no longer works?
- Where have I been spiritually numb, even though I'm physically active?
- What, yes, is God trying to activate in me—but I keep ignoring the nudge?

Your microwave moment is a picture of grace. God doesn't just want you to be aware of your broken patterns, but He wants to renew you through them. You can train your body to reach for what is whole, not what is broken. You can Activate Your Yes in a spiritually grounded and neurologically supported way. Because obedience is more than a decision.

It's a retraining of your desires, your defaults, and your direction.

## WHEN DISOBEDIENCE LOOKS LIKE DISCERNMENT

Looking back at my own faith journey, I now realize that I had trained myself to hesitate, to delay, and to negotiate with God. Honestly, I had learned to give Him a sophisticated no.

Not a loud one. Not outright rebellion. But a refined no. The kind that says, "Let me pray about it first."

But God wasn't asking for analysis. He was asking for obedience. Just one obedient step at a time. And I had gotten good at talking myself out of the very things God was calling me into. Can you relate?

## MY DEFAULT WAS NO

As a high-functioning, depressed pastor's wife, I knew how to look good on the outside, try to live up to people's expectations, and try to manage my disobedience. I didn't understand the full weight of surrender.

Surrender isn't a moment; it's a rewiring. It's an embodied, practiced response over time. You don't just decide your way into obedience. You train for it. Because activation doesn't happen when you just know the truth–it happens when you move with it.

And if you've been practicing fear or procrastination, you're not just battling willpower—you're battling deeply formed neural habits.

Neuroscience confirms what Scripture has always taught: your brain is shaped by what you repeatedly do. Pathways form through repetition. Habits become reflexes. Even broken patterns can feel normal. But when your daily obedience aligns with God's truth, your brain and your life begin to reflect the transformation God always intended.

## THE GAP BETWEEN KNOWING AND DOING

When James writes, "But be doers of the word, and not hearers only, deceiving yourselves" (James 1:22), he's not just issuing a warning; he's describing a pattern. It reveals a neurological gap between what we hear and what we do.

And neuroscience backs it up.

You reinforce a disconnect between conviction and action whenever you hear God's word but delay obedience. You're training your brain to normalize hesitation and saying no. That's self-deception.

You think you're following God. But your patterns are still following fear. The longer you wait, the more distant God's voice begins to feel, not because He stopped speaking, but because disobedience dulls discernment.

## GOOD NEWS: OBEDIENCE REWIRES THE BRAIN

Here's the hope. The moment you say yes—even a trembling yes—something shifts. Obedience reactivates spiritual clarity, builds new neural tracks, and realigns you with God's presence and power.

When James says, "Be doers of the word," he's offering a path toward alignment both spiritually and neurologically. A way to live whole, clear, and obedient.

You don't have to be perfect. But you do have to participate. Because transformation doesn't come through intention alone. It comes through obedience in motion.

# Chapter 4

# THE "YES HAND"

## RAISE YOUR HAND

**I want to share a powerful truth with you, something i've personally learned when my mind starts racing and overthinking tries to take hold.** It's simple, but it is a powerful practice. When you intentionally bring your whole self—your body, your attention, and your unwavering trust back into your intimate relationship with God, something miraculous happens. Your very brain begins to rewire itself, paving a path toward deep healing and unwavering hope.

The way your mind processes what's happening around you profoundly shapes how you respond. But when you intentionally slow down, when you truly choose to be present with the Lord, your entire spiritual and emotional posture can shift into a place of peace and power. This isn't just some new idea or a fleeting theory; this is precisely how our Creator, the Almighty God, designed us to operate.

Sometimes, the most profound act of faith, the most spiritual thing you can do, is simply to lift your hand. Do it right there in the middle of your gnawing doubt, your endless delay, or that heavy decision fatigue. As you lift it, declare with conviction, "I am stopping this spiral right now, and I am saying a resounding yes to God's leading!"

This one simple yet mighty move accomplishes two powerful things. First, it sends a clear signal to your mind and spirit: "Stop!" It interrupts the relentless overthinking and silences the whispers of fear. Second, it sends an even clearer message that freedom is yours: "Yes, Lord! I am surrendering to Your divine leading."

I call this powerful practice the YES Hand.

Just think about it. Your hands are always with you and always ready. You don't need to search for the perfect Scripture or find a perfectly quiet sanctuary. Don't get me wrong. Scripture and prayer are essential. But as we come before God, He also gives us practical tools, embodied habits that help us respond to Him in real time. Raising your hand might feel small, but it's a reset. A way to say, "I'm listening."

This isn't about putting on a show for anyone; it's a personal, powerful practice. It's a divine reset. A tangible way to put your obedience into immediate, Spirit-led motion.

**The YES Hand**

Now, let's talk about how to put the YES Hand into action. Start by raising your hand in front of you. This simple action is a cue—a physical reminder that you're choosing presence over panic and alignment over distraction. You don't need the perfect setting or the right words. You just need a small shift in behavior that changes your direction.

With your hand still up, focus on each finger, one at a time. Each finger represents a step in a repeatable rhythm. This rhythm helps you interrupt the noise, reset your focus, and return to what matters. Small habits, practiced consistently, shape your responses over time. You're retraining your mind and body to respond with spiritual clarity.

## THUMB – I WILL NOTICE

Begin with your thumb and simply say, "I will notice." This is not about solving anything. It's about paying attention. Noticing what's stirring beneath the surface without judgment.

What's your body trying to say? What anxious thoughts are looping relentlessly in your mind? Where are you pulling back, hiding, or pretending that everything is fine?

Continue to simply become aware. You don't have to fix anything here. You're simply letting God into the places you usually try to manage on your own. Overthinking often lurks in the shadows, operating in the background of your mind. But this is your powerful moment to bring it into the light of God's presence.

You cannot walk into healing by pretending it's not there. When you notice what's happening with raw honesty and deep compassion for yourself, you create a sacred space. In that space, you give the Holy Spirit full permission to meet you exactly where you are, with tenderness and grace, allowing you to simply be. This initial step is never about fixing anything; it is purely about honest awareness.

- **Phrases you can say:**

"I notice this tightness in my chest right now."

"I notice this thought of 'I'm not good enough' keeps playing in my head."

"I notice I'm avoiding that important phone call."

"I notice a feeling of overwhelm settling deep within my spirit."

"I notice my mind racing uncontrollably about tomorrow's challenges."

"I notice a strong pull to hide from this difficult situation."

"I notice I'm trying to control something that is truly beyond my reach."

"I notice the weariness that has settled into my very soul."

## POINTER FINGER – I WILL NAME IT

Now, point your finger and declare, “I will name it.” This is your moment to get profoundly honest with yourself and with God. You are calling out, by name, what has been secretly running beneath the surface of your thoughts and emotions. Understand this truth: what you refuse to name, you will unknowingly continue to nurture, allowing it to grow in the shadows. So be bold. Name that fear that's been gripping you. Name the relentless pressure you feel. Name the deep need to control, the perfectionism that binds you, or the heavy weight of shame.

This powerful act is not about labeling yourself or condemning the part of you God is still forming. It is solely about identifying precisely what is getting in the way of your yes to God. When you name it, you reclaim your God-given authority over it.

Be careful to not let shame grow as you name these things. The goal of this step is to bring you back to your center, rooted in Christ. It swings open the door to liberating truth. You stop negotiating with the confusion that has held you captive, and you start stepping boldly into the truth of what God says. While clarity may not always make the next step easy, it absolutely makes it visible.

- **Phrases you can say:**

"I name this fear of failure that's been holding me back."

"I name this spirit of comparison that tries to steal my joy."

"I name this deep need for control that makes me anxious."

"I name this procrastination that keeps me from moving forward."

"I name this feeling of inadequacy that whispers I'm not enough."

"I name this shame from my past that tries to define me."

"I name this anxiety about the future that robs my peace."

"I name this bitterness I've been holding onto in my heart."

## MIDDLE FINGER – I INTERRUPT IT

Now, move to your middle finger and declare with conviction, “I interrupt it!”

This is the powerful moment where you halt the spiral with a deliberate, divine interruption. You are actively interrupting the lie that has held you captive, the shame that has weighed you down, and the relentless pressure that has driven you. You are re-centering your mind, not with human force or fear, but with the unwavering power of God's truth. This is where your yes to God begins to take deep root.

You have been given a voice, and you get to use it to speak directly to the disempowering pattern that has been trying to control your steps. Remind it, with divine authority, that it does not get the final say in your life. This is the moment you courageously refuse to let that old, worn-out script keep running your life. You don't just ignore the troubling thought; you face it head-on, empowered by the Spirit of God. Declare with conviction: "I am going to fight this disempowering thought with the very power of God! This thought is not the truth. This feeling is not my final authority. This old pattern does not get to decide what I do next!"

- **Phrases you can say:**

"I interrupt this lie with the truth of God's Word."

"This fear has no power over me; I am covered by grace."

"I refuse to let worry control my mind or my actions."

"I am breaking agreement with this shame right now, in Jesus' name."

"I am not defined by my past mistakes; I am redeemed and new."

"This pressure is not from God, and I release it to Him completely."

"I am choosing faith over fear at this very moment."

"My identity is firmly rooted in Christ, not in this disempowering thought."

## RING FINGER – I WILL ANCHOR IN TRUTH

This is where you stop reacting to the chaos and realign your spirit with the Lord. To do this, you must immediately insert at least one foundational truth from God's Word. As you touch your ring finger, declare, "I anchor in truth!" Now, choose one powerful truth to hold onto and insert today. Perhaps you say, "Obedience is my truest worship to God". Or, "I was truly made for this very moment." Or even, "I move with the guidance of the Holy Spirit, not with the crushing weight of pressure." This is the moment you courageously refuse to let the old, disempowering script keep running your life.

You don't ignore the troubling thought; you face it head-on with the power of God's Word. After interrupting the lie, your very nervous system needs something steady and true to hold onto. This is precisely where you firmly align yourself with your unshakable identity in Christ Jesus, rather than being swayed by the whispers of insecurity.

- **Phrases you can say:**

"I am a child of God, deeply loved and fully accepted by Him."

"God's grace is more than sufficient for me in every situation."

"The Lord is my Shepherd; I shall not want for anything I truly need."

"I can do all things through Christ who strengthens me from within."

"God has not given me a spirit of fear, but of power, of love, and of a sound mind."

"I am fearfully and wonderfully made in His image and likeness."

"His mercies are new every single morning; great is His faithfulness."

"I am more than a conqueror through Him who loves me unconditionally."

## PINKY FINGER – I WILL MOVE

Now, move to your pinky finger and ask yourself this powerful question: "What is one small, Spirit-led act of obedience I can take right now?"

- Perhaps it's sending that text message to the person you've been avoiding.

- Maybe it's finally hitting 'send' on that important email.
- It could be simply starting that first page of your project.
- It might be having that difficult but necessary conversation.
- Or perhaps it's just praying that prayer you've been putting off.

The pinky finger may seem small, but it powerfully completes this divine rhythm. This is the triumphant moment you declare, “I am not just thinking about change; I am actively living it!”

## YOUR YES IS IN YOUR HAND

Every single time you raise your hand, you are accomplishing two profound things. You are decisively stopping the spiral of overthinking and fear, and you are powerfully declaring your Yes to God's leading.

You do not need a perfect, meticulously planned strategy. What you truly need is a faithful, intentional pause. And here's the liberating truth: you already possess everything you need, placed within you by God, to take your very next step.

So when fear starts creeping in and you feel it tightening your chest, when your thoughts are racing faster than your prayers, when you’re unsure, unqualified, and everything in you wants to shrink back—pause.

Lift your hand.

Let it be your quiet declaration that God is still in control.
Let it be your way of saying yes to His call, even when your confidence is shaking.

Because obedience doesn't always feel bold. Sometimes, it's simply choosing to move forward while the fear is still talking. That's what an activated Yes looks like.

# Chapter 5

# POWERFUL RHYTHMS FOR AN ACTIVATED LIFE

**You've just walked through the YES Hand, a powerful, Spirit-led rhythm that helps you respond in real time to fear, overthinking, and spiritual resistance.** But here's the truth: lasting transformation doesn't come from one moment alone. It comes from rhythms.They are intentional, repeated choices that shape your spiritual reflexes over time. If the YES Hand helps you stop the spiral in a single moment, then these next rhythms will help yousustain your Yes day by day.

Let's take what you've started in your hand and build it into your life.

The first rhythm is one you can begin practicing immediately, no matter your schedule or setting.

1. **The Rhythm of Intentional Pause (Daily):**

○ **What it is:** This isn't just stopping; it's stopping *with purpose*. It's carving out a non-negotiable moment, even just five minutes, to intentionally disconnect from the noise and reconnect with God. This could be your YES Hand Practice, a moment of silent breathing, or simply acknowledging God's presence.

○ **Why it works:** In our hyper-stimulated world, constant activity can deafen us to the Holy Spirit's whispers. An intentional pause creates space for clarity, allowing your nervous system to settle and your spirit to hear. It's a deliberate act of choosing presence over performance.

○ **How it feels:** Like taking a deep, cleansing breath in a chaotic room. It might feel awkward at first, but it quickly becomes essential for spiritual oxygen.

**2. The Rhythm of Truth Infusion (Daily/Weekly):**

○ **What it is:** Actively feeding your spirit with God's Word. This means more than just reading; it's meditating on scripture, listening to biblically sound teaching, and journaling what God reveals. It's about saturating your mind with what is true, lovely, and excellent (Philippians 4:8).

○ **Why it works:** Lies, fear, and self-doubt thrive in a vacuum of truth. Consistent truth infusion rewires your thinking, strengthening your spiritual immune system against the enemy's whispers. It builds a solid foundation for your identity in Christ.

○ **How it feels:** Like drinking fresh, cool water when you're parched. It nourishes your soul and brings a deep sense of stability and peace.

**3. The Rhythm of Honest Confession & Forgiveness (As Needed/Regularly):**

○ **What it is:** Acknowledging your shortcomings, your fears, your hidden motives, and receiving His forgiveness. This also extends to forgiving yourself and others who have wounded you.

○ **Why it works:** Unconfessed sin, unaddressed shame, and unforgiveness are spiritual weights that anchor your yes in the past. This rhythm releases those burdens, creating freedom and lightness for movement. It's a vital part of spiritual hygiene.

○ **How it feels:** Like a heavy backpack being lifted from your shoulders.It might sting to be honest at first, but the relief and freedom that follow are profound.

**4. The Rhythm of Small, Obedient Steps (Daily):**

○ **What it is:** Identifying and taking that "next Yes"—the one small, tangible action God is prompting you to do right now, even if it feels insignificant or scary. This is your "Pinky Finger" in action.

○ **Why it works:** Momentum builds through consistency, not perfection. Each small act of obedience builds spiritual muscle and trust in God's leading. It dismantles the overwhelm of a grand vision into manageable, powerful increments.

○ **How it feels:** Like a tiny spark igniting a flame. Each step builds confidence and reveals the path forward, proving that God is truly with you.

**5. The Rhythm of Grateful Declaration (Daily):**

○ **What it is:** Intentionally focusing on and articulating what you are grateful for, even in challenging circumstances. This moves beyond just a feeling to an active declaration of God's goodness.

○ **Why it works:** Gratitude shifts your perspective from lack to abundance, from fear to faith. It cultivates a spirit of contentment and joy, which are powerful fuel for an activated life. It acknowledges God's faithfulness in the past and present.

○ **How it feels:** Like a warm glow spreading through your spirit, chasing away shadows. It opens your eyes to blessings you might otherwise miss.

**6. The Rhythm of Community Connection (Weekly/Regularly):**

○ **What it is:** Actively engaging with a faith-filled community that encourages, challenges, and supports your Activated Yes journey. This means being present, vulnerable, and accountable.

○ **Why it works:** You were not designed to do this alone. An authentic community provides strength, perspective, and a mirror for your growth. It offers a safe space to share struggles and celebrate victories, preventing isolation which can stifle your "yes."

○ **How it feels:** Like finding your tribe, a place where you are truly seen, heard, and championed. It provides the spiritual oxygen and accountability needed for sustained movement.

These rhythms are not rigid rules but invitations to a dance with the Holy Spirit. As you begin to incorporate even one or two of them consistently, you will witness your Yes transform from a quiet whisper into a powerful, unstoppable force in your life. A word of caution: Don't let these rhythms become checklists that pull you into performance mode. Let them guide you into a deeper encounter with the God who is already working within you.

## Soul Check-ins

These questions are designed to help you identify the hidden "nos" in your life—the subtle ways you resist God's invitation to activate your "Yes." Approach these with a spirit of honesty and a desire for liberation, knowing that confronting your "no" is the first step toward profound freedom and movement.

1. The Hidden "No": Beyond the obvious, where do you find yourself subtly saying "no" to God's promptings, even if you don't voice it out loud?
2. The Root of Resistance: What is the deepest fear or insecurity that fuels your "no"?
3. "Hiding Behind" Tactics: How do you typically "hide" or rationalize your "no"? Do you delay obedience by saying "I'll pray about it" indefinitely, or by getting caught up in busyness that avoids the real issue?
4. The Cost of Your "No": How has your "no" to God's promptings chipped away at your joy, peace, or sense of purpose in the past?
5. The Invitation to Surrender: What is one specific "no" that God is inviting you to confront and surrender today?

Chapter 6

# WHERE MY YES BEGAN

**We've just walked through some rhythms that can change your life.** But here's what you need to know: I didn't start there. Long before there was a book or a framework or any clarity at all, I was stuck. Overwhelmed. Ashamed of what I hadn't accomplished and afraid of what I still felt called to do.

The journey to an activated yes wasn't neat. It wasn't fast. It came through doubt, failure, and a thousand small decisions that felt like they wouldn't matter, but they did. I had to learn that obedience doesn't always look like bold confidence. Sometimes it looks like whispering yes when everything in you wants to run.

So before we step into the heart of the YES Framework, I want to take you back. Not for the sake of looking behind, but so you understand where this came from and what's possible when God meets you in your mess.

## IT DIDN'T START WITH A YES

I didn't wake up one day and decide to write a book called Activate Your Yes. It didn't come in a moment of clarity or during a clean season of victory. This book was born out of pain. It was carved out of personal failure—failure I thought I'd take to my grave.

This isn't just a message. It's the result of two decades of learning to follow God one trembling step at a time.

If you had met me twenty-five years ago, you wouldn't have found a woman on fire for God. You would have met a woman slowly fading beneath silent disappointment, unhealed wounds, and buried embarrassment. I was doing ministry, but underneath the smile lived deep insecurity and soul-level exhaustion.

My depression didn't look like sadness. It looked like what I thought was normal: overwhelm, overcommitment, and burnout. I had lost track of who I was and whose I was. I didn't feel I had much to offer God or the world.

I carried quiet shame that I should've been further along by now. More accomplished. More successful. More something. At 28, I still hadn't finished college. I didn't have a title, a résumé, or a professional identity. I was doing sacred work—raising children, serving people—but I didn't think any of it counted.

Then one day, I received an invitation to my high school reunion. I remember holding the envelope and wondering, "What would I say if I showed up?". "What do I have to show for my life?". I couldn't see it clearly then, but I was chasing validation. I was trying to prove I mattered.

I wanted success. But what I really wanted was approval. I thought if I could build something successful, I could silence the voice in my head that kept saying I wasn't enough.

## I TRIED TO BUILD MY WAY OUT OF SHAME

So, I came up with an idea: I should start a business. It made sense. I loved fashion, had a vision, and had good credit at the time. I convinced my husband to invest. While he wasn't fully on board, he believed in me, and that was enough for me.

Shortly after, I opened a resale/retail boutique almost three hours from home. I had employees, a building, and the belief that I could create something beautiful. I was excited, committed, and a visionary.

But here's what I didn't know: Knowing how to pick good clothes doesn't mean you know how to run a business. There were so many things I hadn't planned for: Inventory. Marketing. Payroll. Taxes. Rent. Utilities. Systems. Processes.

I was operating on grit and guesswork. And even though I was working harder than ever, the numbers didn't add up. But I told myself it would turn around. I believed all entrepreneurs went through slow seasons. All I needed was one good month.

But month after month, I kept falling behind. And instead of being honest, I went silent.

## FROM VISION TO SURVIVAL MODE

I didn't want to appear to have failed, not to myself, my husband, or anyone else. So, I started juggling bills. Shuffling accounts. Delaying payments and quietly slipping into survival mode. What began with faith and optimism slowly became desperation.

And that's when compromise started creeping in.

Without realizing it, I began taking shortcuts. I hid the money problems. I told half-truths. I moved money around and tried to "fix" it. I told myself I'd pay it back and that it wasn't really a big deal.

But it was. One day, our church bookkeeper called my husband: the check he had written had bounced. He thought it was a bank error until he went to the bank. And the banker said plainly:

"Sir, your account has been in the red for quite some time." That was the beginning of unraveling the lie I had lived in for four years.

## WHEN THE TRUTH CAME OUT

My husband was shocked. Embarrassed. Hurt. His trust in me as his wife and partner was shattered.

He wasn't just angry. He was blindsided. The man who had always believed the best about me was now staring at a reality he didn't see coming.

I'll never forget the pain in his voice when he asked, "Kim, how could you do this to me?" He didn't yell. He didn't go silent. He was broken. And I sat there, stripped of every defense. There were no words that could undo what I had done. More than the money, my husband was grieving the trust.

I didn't even recognize myself. I had become someone I never thought I could be. Somewhere along the way, I drifted so far from the woman I used to be, the one who wanted to please God and live with integrity. The slow compromise hadn't felt like rebellion at the time.I had convinced myself I was "helping." That it would all work out in the end. But it didn't. I had betrayed God. Betrayed my husband and betrayed myself.

## THE COLLAPSE

The business failed. We filed for bankruptcy. My identity and reputation crumbled. And I felt like I was a total failure. How could this happen to the pastor's wife, the Christian who knew better, the one who preached about faith to others? Shame followed me like a shadow. Guilt whispered in every quiet moment. I wasn't just broken, I was exhausted. Spiritually empty. Emotionally numb. And yet... God met me right there.

Not with condemnation. But with an invitation.

## THE NIGHT EVERYTHING CHANGED

That night, God didn't lecture me. He loved me. He offered restoration and redemption in the very place I had expected judgment. That was the night everything began to shift. I didn't even know it then, but that was my first real Yes. Not a fancy one. Not a public one. But a real one.

A surrendered Yes. A whisper, I'm still willing to follow, even if I'm limping. It didn't fix everything. But it reoriented my soul. It began a new rhythm of healing, listening, rebuilding, and learning to obey in the dark. I started following God the best I knew how.

Sometimes it meant apologizing. Sometimes it meant resting. Sometimes it meant creating. Sometimes it meant confessing. But each act of obedience became a step forward, no matter how small. I didn't realize it then, but I was learning to activate my Yes.

## "HOW DID YOU GO FROM A BREAKDOWN TO A BREAKTHROUGH?"

A woman asked me that question years later. And without overthinking, I said:

"I activated my Yes."

I didn't say it as a catchphrase. It was what I had lived. I wasn't announcing a perfect track record. I was declaring a posture. That phrase came from deep in my spirit and resonated with us both.

That Yes became the turning point.

For the next six months, I couldn't stop saying it. It became my declaration. I'd say it repeatedly everywhere I went: "I'm just activating my Yes." It became the way I stayed grounded in what God was asking of me, even when the road wasn't clear.

Some time later, I was asked by an organization to speak at the Billy Graham Center, and I remember sitting in prayer after that moment, asking, "Lord, what do you want me to say?" I had no interest in impressing anyone. I just wanted to be faithful.

In that quiet time of prayer with God, the answer came clearly:

## TEACH THEM HOW TO ACTIVATE THEIR YES.

The Holy Spirit led me to Acts 9—the story of Ananias. A man who said yes to God, not because he had it all figured out, but because he trusted the One who called him. He wasn't fearless. He was faithful. He didn't obey because it was easy. He obeyed because God said "go". That's what activating your Yes looks like.

## FROM PHRASE TO FRAMEWORK

After that message, over 200 women came up to me and said: "I'm going to activate my Yes." The next morning, God gave me a clear commission: Help as many people as you can before you die to activate their Yes.

So, you see, I didn't invent it. I just named what God was already doing in my life. And I wanted to offer it back as a helpful guide for anyone ready to live their Yes on purpose. What God had been shaping in my life was meant to be shared. Not as a formula, but as a framework. A way to walk with surrender, clarity, and courage, day by day.

So now, let me show you what it looks like to live it out.

# THE YES FRAMEWORK

# PART 1 YIELD TO GOD’S LEADING

# Chapter 7

# SAYING YES WITHOUT THE MAP

**If we are going to activate our yes, we have to first recognize the necessity to yield to Christ.** Most of us already know we're supposed to surrender our lives to Christ. We sing about it. We pray for it. We say we want to follow God wherever He leads.

But if we're honest, many of us are more comfortable with the idea of yielding than the actual practice. The gap between our theological understanding and our daily walk often lies in the fear of the unknown or the reluctance to relinquish control.

## THE PROBLEM: WE WANT CLARITY FIRST

We've grown used to having answers on demand. If we don't know something, we Google it. If we're unsure, we look for steps, signs, or strategies. We need to feel equipped before we finally move.The truth is, clarity doesn't come first. Trust does.

God doesn't say, "Once you understand, then you can obey." He says, "Follow Me."

That's it.

If you're like me, you've probably prayed for a sign or even begged for a feeling. But I've learned this:sometimes God doesn't answer with details; He answers with direction. Clarity is a gift God often gives in motion. So let's get to steppin'!

## THE PATTERN OF SCRIPTURE: TRUST THEN CLARITY

That truth isn't just for your life and my life. It's been there since the beginning of Scripture. I think about when God told Abraham, "Go to the land that I will show you" (Genesis 12:1). He didn't give him a map. He gave him directions.

Abraham's legacy didn't begin because he had all the details. It began because he was willing to yield to the unknown. Romans 4:20 reminds us: "No unbelief made him waver concerning the promise of God, but he grew strong in his faith as he gave glory to God."

Abraham didn't grow strong in the fulfillment; he grew strong in the waiting. While nothing in his body or circumstances confirmed the promise, he yielded his logic to God's Word. And that yielded a legacy formed through faith.That kind of faith isn't just forAbraham; it's for all of us. You don't have to be a spiritual giant. You have to be willing to follow when God speaks.

That's what Abraham did. He wasn't holding onto proof. He was holding onto a promise. He had to let go of evidence and lean into God's character. And as he gave glory to God in the waiting, his faith grew.

Sometimes, God's direction comes as just one word.

Stay.

Forgive.

Speak.

Rest.

Apply.

Wait.

Move.

That one word won't be the full picture, but it's always the right place to start. Obedience is how we follow God's lead. So take the next obedient step. That's how God is honored and breakthroughs begin.

## CONTROL FEELS SAFER BUT IT'S COSTING YOU

The hard part? Trust doesn't feel safe when you're used to controlling the outcome. Trust means you're not the one driving. It means you move even if your hands are shaking.

And yes, it's scary. Because trust isn't natural. Control is. Overthinking is. Delaying is. But trust? That's the beginning of surrender. That's the real yes.

God doesn't need your full understanding. He asks for your full attention.

So, if you wait to feel 100% ready before you obey, you'll be waiting forever. You don't need to feel ready. You need to be willing. And you need to know this: God never asked you to figure it out. That's not your role.

Your role is to trust that the One who calls you is faithful, and He will do it (1 Thessalonians 5:24).

Sometimes, we confuse clarity with safety. We'd finally feel secure if we could see everything. But faith isn't built on what you see, but on who you follow. God doesn't lead like GoogleMaps. He's not trying to give you step 12 before you take step 1. He's trying to *form* you while you walk.

That's why this chapter isn't about having all the answers. It's about becoming a person who says yes without needing them.

### Here's what trust looks like in everyday life:

- Sending the email even if you're scared of rejection.
- Starting the healing conversation, even if your voice trembles.
- Opening your Bible even when you feel numb.
- Praying again after a season of silence.
- Saying yes to the next right thing, not the whole plan.

Trust is often quiet—not a shout, but a whisper: "Okay, God. I'm scared. But I'll go anyway."

And if you're wondering, "What if I miss it?" let me tell you something that took me years to believe: God's voice is not fragile, and your future is not hanging by a thread.

If your heart is set on following God, you must yield to how He wants to lead you through fear and delay.

## SOUL CHECK-IN

Where in your life are you waiting for clarity when God is simply asking for trust?

What would it look like today to move forward, not with a full plan, but with full surrender?

Chapter 8

# GOD'S NOT SLOW, HE'S STRATEGIC

**Let me tell you something I wish I had learned earlier: God doesn't move at the speed of your expectations.** He moves at the pace of your transformation. Yielding will frustrate you if you think it's about getting quicker results. Because sometimes, you're obeying and nothing is changing.

You said yes. You showed up. You're praying. You're trying. And still... the door hasn't opened. The answers haven't come. The situation hasn't shifted. That's where most people walk away—not because they don't love God, but because they can't reconcile His pace with their plan.

I've been there. I remember asking God, "Why is this taking so long?" And deep in my spirit, I sensed Him say:"I'm not slow. I'm strategic." I had to realize: God wasn't ignoring me. He was forming me. And formation takes time. "The Lord is not slow to fulfill his promise as some count slowness, but is patient toward you..." (2 Peter 3:9) God's not stalling. He's preparing. Yielding is not about speed. It's about submission.

And sometimes the greatest miracle is not in what changes around you, but in what shifts within you.

I didn't know it at the time, but when I was in my longest waiting season, God was strengthening my trust muscles. He was teaching me how to walk without knowing what was ahead, how to release the deadlines I had placed on my own healing, and how to stop striving and start listening.

That's what yielding does. It pulls you out of urgency and places you into God's rhythm. And here's what I've learned in that rhythm:

- Delayed is not denied.
- Stillness is not stuck.
- Quiet does not mean God is absent.

It often means He's closer than you realize, doing something in you that will sustain what He wants to do through you.

### That shows up in real life like this:

- Not forcing a job change because you're bored—waiting until you're released, not just restless.
- Staying in counseling even when you're tempted to run.
- Refusing to compare your pace to someone else's breakthrough.
- Choosing prayer over panic when your timeline feels off.
- Trusting that God's delays are never empty. He fills them with preparation.

When I look back, some of my most painful seasons were the ones where God was most preparing me. I thought I was being overlooked, but I was being realigned. I thought God was late, but He was right on time for something I couldn't yet see. So, if you're in a season that feels slow, let me say this to you:

God is not trying to rush you. He's trying to root you. And that's what yielding looks like in real life. Not just trusting God's yes or no, but trusting His timing. It means walking in step with a Savior who's more interested in your formation than your speed. Because when you yield to His pace, you don't just arrive–you grow into the kind of person who's ready when you get there. And when you do, you'll realize the wait was part of the preparation.

# PART 2: EMBODY THE CHARACTER OF CHRIST

Chapter 9

# THE FIRE OF FORMATION

**Years ago, I'll never forget this one Easter Sunday.** If you've ever led in the church you know it's our Super Bowl moment—the day Jesus defeated sin, Satan, and the grave.

At the time, I was the worship leader. I knew I had a big responsibility to help guide people into the presence of God on one of the most significant Sundays of the year. The worship space was full, the music was powerful, and everyone was dressed in their best. I was on cloud nine, ready to give God my all.

But even as I smiled and served, there was something unsettled in the background. Over the past few weeks, there had been tension between me and our pianist. Nothing explosive—just quiet friction around music choices, communication, and leadership dynamics. We hadn't addressed it fully, but I chalked it up to the usual growing pains of team ministry. I assumed we were still okay.

I was wrong.

During our regular meet-and-greet time—I took a quick moment to say hello to the pianist. I walked over to her, smiled, and said, "I'll see you Tuesday night at rehearsal."

She paused and looked me dead in the eye and said, "I quit."

She didn't explain. She just went back to the keyboard and sat down.

My heart sank. I stood there in shock, blindsided. Of all the moments she could have told me she was quitting, she chose this one. Not just any Sunday—but Resurrection Sunday. I didn't know what to do. I could roll my eyes. Let bitterness bubble up. Say something petty to match the moment. But deep in the swirl of emotions, I heard the Holy Spirit whisper: "I'm here with you. This is the moment you get to look like Jesus."

I ran to the bathroom just a few feet away, locked myself in a stall, and sobbed. It was one of those ugly cries, but I had 90 seconds before the next song started so I had to get it together fast.

But even in just that short time, something shifted. It was a call to look more like Jesus and less like me. I felt God's presence that steadied me. I walked out of that bathroom knowing I wasn't alone. I nodded to the sound person to cue the track. The song? "It Wasn't Easy, But It Was Worth It" by CeCe Winans.

Tell me God doesn't have a sense of humor.

That moment became a marker in my life. While I was still crying and singing, I thought of Philippians 3:10: "That I may know him and the power of his resurrection, and may share his sufferings, becoming like him in his death." The congregation didn't see that I wasn't just worshiping, I was being formed. Sometimes formation looks like worship on the outside and breaking on the inside.

Here's what I've learned from that Easter and many moments like it. Resurrection power doesn't usually show up without something in us first dying. It might be your pride. You need to be in control. Your desire to defend yourself. Your old way of reacting. Here's the thing, reflecting Christ's character doesn't happen without the cross.

Jesus said in Luke 9:23,"If anyone would come after me, let him deny himself and take up his cross daily and follow me."

This is what spiritual formation looks like. This formation can happen in the most ordinary place. In a church hallway, a boardroom, in the line at the grocery store. Or right in the middle of your kitchen. Wherever it is, you'll be given a choice: Will you react from your flesh, or respond from the Spirit?

That Easter Sunday became a class room of Christlike character for me. I was being conformed, shaped, and formed intoHis likeness, not through applause, but through pain. Romans 8:29 tells us,

"For those whom he foreknew he also predestined to be conformed to the image of his Son..." That's what was happening to me.I wasn't just leading worship; I was being led into transformation. God wasn't asking me to be perfect. He was asking me to stay present. To yield in the tension. To trust Him with my tears.

So many of us love the idea of looking like Christ. But are sometimes resistant or hesitant when the lessons are through disappointment, discomfort, conflict, obscurity, or silence.

*That*'s where you learn to look like Jesus. Although one of my forming moments happened while leading in a church capacity, spiritual maturity isn't solely forged in public ministry. It's also in those everyday moments that test our character when no one is watching.

## This Is What It Looks Like to Embody Christ

Here's what it often looks like when Christ's character starts showing up in your life: When You Embody Christ's Character, You Might...

- Speak truth in love, even when it would be easier to go silent or lash out.
- Stay present in pain, not because it's easy, but because the Spirit has anchored you.
- Choose patience when someone's words cut deep.
- Say no to control, and yes to compassion.
- Forgive when you'd rather defend.
- Let humility lead instead of pride proving a point.
- Bless those who blindsided you.
- Tell the truth, not to get revenge, but to create restoration.
- Worship with tears still fresh from the blow no one else saw.

This isn't weakness. This is what Dallas Willard would call the renovation of the heart. It's spiritual maturity—formed in the quiet, costly moments when no one else may be clapping, but God is watching. Colossians 3:12 reminds us,

"Put on then, as God's chosen ones, holy and beloved, compassionate hearts, kindness, humility, meekness, and patience..." But let's be clear: You don't reflect Christ by trying harder. You don't become like Jesus by forcing yourself to be "nice." You don't mature spiritually by stuffing your emotions and talking through gritted teeth.

> The power to look like Jesus doesn't come from your willpower. It comes from His Spirit shaping your soul.

Galatians 2:20 says, "It is no longer I who live, but Christ who lives in me." That's the secret.

You don't become like Jesus through striving. You become like Him through surrender. When you say yes to His character, God supplies the power. When you yield, He forms you. When you step out in obedience, He meets you in that moment.

## CHURCH WAS OVER, BUT MY SURRENDER WASN'T

After the service ended.I didn't approach the pianist, not because I avoided her, but because the Spirit led me to be still. Truthfully, I was still raw, wounded, and shaken. I smiled and talked to everyone else, but inside, I was replaying the entire encounter.

When I got in the car with my husband, the tears flowed. My husband noticed immediately and gently asked what happened. As I explained, the pain sat heavy in my chest. But even through the ache, I knew God wasn't just forming something in me—He was calling me to respond like Him.

The next day, I picked up the phone. Not to fix it. Not to convince her to stay. But to follow Jesus' instruction in Matthew 18:15: "If your brother sins against you, go and tell him his fault, between you and him alone..." I called and asked if we could meet that week. She agreed.

It was a hard—but—honest conversation. I told her how much her words had hurt and how the timing crushed me. She apologized for how she handled it. And I chose forgiveness.

Now let me pause and say this: forgiveness is rarely one clean moment. That day, I decided to walk in the direction of healing. No drama. No bitterness. No spiritual bypassing. Just honest obedience.

Letting God's grace and truth begin to heal the wound in my soul. She left the church.(Let's just say—I didn't throw her a going-away party.) But there was no resentment in my heart.

Here's what I want you to hear: Embodying the character of Christ isn't about getting the outcome you want. It's about becoming the person God is shaping you to be. This is what the "E" in YES is all about. It's not a personality upgrade. It's spiritual formation. You're not performing for God. You're becoming like Him.

I learned something that day, and it's stayed with me: It's in the crucible of life that God forms us most. Not in comfort. Not in applause. But in the hardest, most unseen, most soul-revealing places.

That's where formation happens.

And that's what turns ordinary obedience into a life-changing story.

# SOUL CHECK-IN

Pause here. Take a breath. These questions are an invitation to be honest with God and yourself as you learn to embody Christ in real life.

1. Where is God inviting you to beJesus with skin on to reflect His heart through your actions?

2. What's one relationship where you can choose humility over defensiveness, or gentleness over control?

3. Who around you needs to encounter Christ, not just in words, but in your presence, patience, or perseverance?

4. When life presses in, who do you want people to experience–more of Christ, or more of you?

# Chapter 10

# BECOMING LIKE CHRIST IN REAL LIFE

**Embodying Christ's character doesn't stop at conflict resolution or relationship repair.** It reaches into every part of life.

Most of us admire the idea of becoming like Jesus, but we don't always realize what it actually takes. We picture transformation happening through big spiritual moments, but real formation often happens in the small, unnoticed ones.

This is where the Spirit does His slow, invisible work of formation. When Jesus said, "One who is faithful in a very little is also faithful in much" (Luke 16:10), He wasn't talking about fame.He was talking about the sacredness of the small.

This is where many people get stuck. They think embodying Christ is about rising to the moment when the stakes are high. But it's really about how you carry yourself in the day-to-day. When someone disappoints you. When no one thanks you. When you're tempted to cut corners, avoid responsibility, or just go with what's easy. In those moments, your instincts reveal your maturity. Formation isn't just about what you know but also in how you respond.

## BUILDING THE MUSCLE OF DAILY OBEDIENCE

So what does this actually look like in real life?

This isn't about becoming legalistic or performance-driven. It's about understanding that consistency *is* formation. Responding with a daily yes is what keeps your Yes from just being an emotional moment and turns it into a way of living. For example, let's say you feel called to write a book, launch a business, start mentoring others. The natural instinct is to wait for a breakthrough moment: more time, more clarity, more confidence. But daily obedience asks a different question: *What's the one step of faithfulness I can take today?*

This doesn't start with a major leap. It starts with a single question:

What's the next right Yes I need to give God?

Don't overthink it. If you're waiting on clarity to act, you're probably stalling your formation. God tends to form us through the doing, not before it.

That means instead of asking, "*What's the full five-year plan?*" The better question is, "*What do I need to do today?*"

Many people don't move forward in their calling not because they don't love God but because they never built the muscle of daily obedience. They want to be faithful in the "much," but they've never submitted to being faithful in the "little."

That's not judgment. That's just a real place I think all of us have been.

## Becoming Before Doing: Why Who You Are Matters More Than What You Produce

Before we rush into Step Forward withBoldness, let's pause. Because for many of us, the moment we think about sayingYes to God, our minds race toward doing. What's the next big assignment?

What's the next launch?

What should I build, start, or promote?

But here's something I've learned the hard way: Sometimes, the most spiritual thing you can do is to be still and let God finish forming what He started inside you. I used to be addicted to "what's next." The next event. The next book. The next ministry move. I knew how to serve.

Then one day, the Holy Spirit whispered: Before you go try to change the world, let God change you. That may not look exciting. It may look quiet. Hidden. Unnoticed. You may feel unseen. Uncelebrated. But listen, God sees everything He's forming in you. And He's not wasting a single moment. Let me encourage you to pause the rush. Let God finish what He started. Hidden doesn't mean forgotten. In the quiet, God is crafting someone who can carry the weight of the next Yes.

# SOUL CHECK-IN

1. What's one simple area where you know your yes is required right now? Don't overthink it or over spiritualize it.
2. What is the one small yes you will commit to acting on today, knowing it's building the muscle for your greater calling?
3. Who would benefit as you move into what God already placed within you?

# PART 3 STEP FORWARD WITH BOLDNESS

Chapter 11

# FAITH IN THEORY VS. FAITH IN MOTION

**So far, we've explored Yield and Embody, the first two parts of the YES Framework. Now, it's time to Step.**

For most of my Christian journey, I had faith in theory but not faith in motion. My theology didn't have feet on it. What I didn't know was this: A yes to God that's not lived out eventually becomes activity wrapped in disobedience. Truth that is not practiced becomes weightless. Transformation requires movement. Obedience is not a feeling you wait for, it's a step you take even when clarity is incomplete. If your faith feels stuck, it's not because you're missing information. It's because your formation has stalled where your obedience stopped. It is always time to obey God– not because you have all the answers, but because you trust the One who already gave the invitation.

## Mission Starts in the Hidden Places

As I was coming out of my depression, I was hungry for purpose. I thought God was going to open the door wide for the dreamHe placed in my heart to speak a message of deliverance across the country.

I had gone through the fire, and I thought this was the moment He would showcase the miracle.

But instead, I found myself working for a woman who had contracts with daycares, teaching children through music, because music helps accelerate the learning process.

Seriously, God? You mean to tell me you didn't open the door for me to be a guest speaker or a featured seminar leader... but a music teacher. That wasn't my ambition.

The door you opened for me was a seat on the floor with four-year-olds singing the alphabet and wiping noses during circle time. No mic. No spotlight. No applause. Just little hands, tiny voices, and a blue carpet with kiddie designs on it.

And I remember thinking, "Lord, seriously? This can't be it." But it was. That was the mission. And it was the exact place God needed to rebuild me.

At the time, I didn't know God was answering the very prayer I had prayed. I said, "Use me." I said, "I'll go wherever You send me." But I expected the assignment to look... bigger, more visible, and more strategic.

Instead, He gave me something holy wrapped in something humbling. He gave me an assignment without a platform. I didn't realize it then, but God wasn't delaying me. He was developing me. Hewas pruning pride. Testing my posture. Breaking the need to be seen. Sometimes, the mission of God doesn't start with a moment; it starts with a mindset.

## Identity Before Assignment

I thought I was ready for my assignment. But what I needed was to get rooted in my identity.

The daycare didn't feel "spiritual."It didn't feel like a ministry. But God used it to expose how much of my worth was still attached to visibility. If I wasn't being noticed, I questioned whether I had value. But God doesn't call you to something just to validate you. He calls you to be formed into His image. Obscurity isn't punishment; it's often the place where God purifies your motives and detangles your identity from applause.

Before Jesus performed a miracle, the Father said, "You are my beloved Son; with you I am well pleased" (Mark 1:11).

Identity, then assignment.

That daycare season stripped me in the best way. It silenced the noise, removed the pressure, and brought me back to the core of who I was without titles, stages, or applause.

The kids didn't care about my résumé. They just cared that I showed up, that I was kind, and that I was loving as I sang songs and led them through music. I believe that was the real test all along. Looking like Jesus when no one's watching.

## The Assignment You Didn't Ask For

This was the assignment I didn't ask for. I didn't pray to have a boss who was unfair, unsaved, and unkind. I didn't want the hardest classrooms or the most difficult kids. But because I was her best worker, she gave me the assignments no one else wanted. And still, God was using it. Not to showcase my gifts, but to shape my character.

One day, after leaving yet another daycare she'd assigned me to, one heavier and more demanding than what she gave the others, I'd had enough. I told myself, If she gives me one more assignment, I'm done. A few days later, while I was driving, she called. "I've got another center for you," she said. I clenched the phone in my hand. I told her I'd call her back once I got home. What I didn't say was that I had already decided I was going to quit.

And I didn't plan to go quietly.

I was going to let her know exactly how unfair she'd been, how I felt overlooked, overworked, and completely disrespected. But right before I could pick up the phone to call her back, theHoly Spirit interrupted me. Not with a loud voice, but with a deep inner knowing: Your assignment is not over.

I froze. Tears welled up. Disappointment filled my heart. What do you do when the very place you want to leave is the one God is leading you to stay?

I had been asking for a release, but God was looking for my obedience. In that moment, I realized obedience wouldn't look like escape. It would look like surrender.

So, I stayed. Not because it was easy. But because it was obedience. That job became my altar. That classroom became my training ground. I stopped working for a paycheck. I started working with a purpose and a perspective to give God the highest glory. The assignment didn't feel glorious.

But it was forming something in me that I would need later, when the mic came, the crowd showed up, and the pressure increased.

Obedience isn't always glamorous. Sometimes it looks like staying put. Sometimes it looks like singing songs you don't feel like singing, and being faithful in the dark.

God wasn't trying to see what I could produce. He was teaching me how to work as unto the Lord. And He was also teaching me how to worship and Honor Him through difficulty and uncomfortability. It was in this season of my life that God reminded me that a true Yes doesn't begin when it's convenient, it begins when it's costly.

## What I Know Now

I thought I was stuck. But I wasn't stuck, I was sent. God was not trying to delay my purpose. He was reshaping my heart. I had been treating my Yes like a spotlight. But God was treating it like a seed. A seed that had to die before it could grow (John 12:24). A seed that needed to stay hidden so it could be strong. And now I know: The mission doesn't begin when you feel ready. It begins when you stop resisting where God has placed you. The Mission Was Never Meant to Be distant or disconnected from your real life.

When you said yes to Jesus, you didn't just agree to salvation; you entered a mission, not a distant, abstract one, but one that starts where your feet are.

God's mission is not reserved for pastors, missionaries, or church planters. It's for every believer. It's for you. The mission is the gospel. The invitation is discipleship. The command is to go and make more disciples. "Go therefore and make disciples of all nations, baptizing them... teaching them to observe all that I have commanded you."
—(Matthew 28:19–20)

You don't have to fly overseas to fulfill the Great Commission. You just have to obey where you are. I Didn'tKnow the Daycare Was a Mission Field.

My season of working at the daycare stripped me of ego. Why? There was no applause, no spiritual accolades, just children learning how to sing and learn about music while God was re-teaching me, His beloved daughter.

He was forming me for something more eternal than a stage. That daycare didn't delay my destiny. It revealed it.

## You Are Already Sent

I love this verse: "As the Father has sent me, even so I am sending you." (John 20:21)

That verse always re-centers me. TheGreek word for “sent” here is “apostellō.” It means to be dispatched with purpose. That means wherever you are right now, there is a purpose. You’re not just passing time. You’re participating in the gospel story.

Let’s make this clear: God’s mission is to reconcile people to Himself through Christ, and He chooses to use His people to do it. He sends us to make disciples.

I used to think disciple-making required degrees or deep theological training. But what I’ve learned is that discipleship is not about perfection. It’s about presence. It’s about walking with someone while you’re still growing. “We are ambassadors for Christ, God making his appeal through us...” (2 Corinthians 5:20)

You don’t need a mic. You need a willing heart. Discipleship starts with who’s already in your life.

That doesn’t always involve preaching. Often, it involves listening, showing up, serving faithfully, and loving consistently. It can also involve raising kids, caring for aging parents, mentoring a teen, inviting a friend to church, or forgiving someone who never said sorry.

This is the mission of God: to draw all people to Himself through the witness of those who have already been changed by grace.

## Trust the Process: A Cohort Story

When I joined a ministry leadership cohort in Atlanta, the regional director's rallying phrase was simple: "Trust the process." Everyone in that room knew those words well. Our cohort consisted of leaders from all kinds of backgrounds and experiences. We didn't always understand the assignments we were given, or the pace God was leading us through, but that phrase kept echoing: Trust the process.

Looking back, I see how true that was. God knows what He's doing with your "Yes." His process does not always make sense to us, but God knows what He's doing. And just like our cohort, every believer who makes up the Church comes from different places, with different callings, but we're part of one mission. The gospel unites us.

Mission Isn't a Stage. It's a Posture. We have to stop treating God's mission like a moment we graduate into.Mission is not a stage. It's not an event. It's not a five-year plan. Mission is how you respond to where God has already placed you.

It's seeing your kitchen table as a holy altar. It's realizing the workplace conflict is an opportunity to embody grace. It's noticing the grocery store cashier and choosing to smile with intention. It's understanding that every interaction is spiritual, even if it looks ordinary.

God doesn't need perfect conditions. He needs your participation. You're Not Just Called to Something—You're Called to Someone The gospel is not a task list. It's a relationship that reshapes everything. God's mission isn't about productivity—it's about presence. Before Jesus sent the disciples out, He first called them to Himself. "He appointed twelve so that they might be with him and he might send them out...(Mark 3:14)

Be with Him first. That's the rhythm of the mission. From intimacy flows impact. You don't work for love. You work from it. Your Everyday Life Is a Discipleship Platform.

That daycare job? It was about more than kids. It was about coworkers watching how I handled pressure. It was the parents who noticed my kindness on hard days. It was my character being tested in secret.

Some of your most powerful gospel moments will come when you least expect them. "Only let your manner of life be worthy of the gospel of Christ..." (Philippians 1:27) That doesn't mean perfection. It means integrity. It means your message and your manner match.

It looks like:

- Listening before reacting.
- Pausing before posting.
- Forgiving when it would feel easier to rehearse the offense.
- Saying "I was wrong."
- Showing up to a hard conversation with grace and truth.
- Making that phone call you've been avoiding.
- Following the Holy Spirit's nudge when you weren't planning to be interrupted.

Disciple-making requires obedience, not degrees or deep theological training. Discipleship is about walking with someone while you're still growing. "We are ambassadors for Christ, God making his appeal through us..." (2 Corinthians 5:20). You don't need a mic. You need a willing heart. Discipleship starts with who's already in your life.

# SOUL CHECK-IN

Let's pause here for a moment of reflection.

Ask yourself:

1. How might your current season–no matter how hidden or hard–be part of God's greater mission through you?
2. Who are you intentionally helping grow in Christ right now? And what's one way you can show up for them this week?
3. Is there a place in your life where you are resisting the mission because it doesn't feel "big enough"?
4. How might my ordinary obedience open the door for someone else's transformation?

## Chapter 12

# GOD'S MISSION IS IN THE THRIFT STORE TOO

Yes, I've spoken from platforms, led teams, and launched books. But I've also shared the gospel in a thrift store line. I've encouraged a mom while flipping through garage sale bins. I've talked about Jesus while sorting through $3 jackets.

God is teaching me wherever I go, I carry the mission. You don't need perfect conditions to be on a mission. You need a heart that says: "Here I am. Use me." You're Holding the Gospel in both your heart and your hand–what a joy to release it through your voice and your story.

Look at your life like a portfolio of gospel potential. Your time. Your gifts. Your experiences. Your pain. Your work. Your family. Your neighborhood. None of it is random. God wants to use all of it to reach someone else. So, the question isn't, "What can I build?" The question is, "What have I been given?" And, "Am I willing to say Yes to it?"

### YOUR MISSION IS ALREADY IN MOTION

Please hear my heart right now. You don't need to wait until you feel ready. The Great Commission isn't a future assignment;

it's a present call. Wherever you are. Whatever you're doing. Whoever is around you. That's your mission field. And when you say Yes to that, you're stepping into the veryheart of God.

For many of us, especially those with a burning desire to create, to lead, to impact, we often fall into the trap of waiting. We wait for the perfect platform, the ideal budget, the "right" credentials, or that grand, undeniable sign. We believe our mission can only truly begin when all the pieces are perfectly aligned, when we feel completely ready and equipped. But here's the liberating truth: **your mission is not a future event; it is already in motion right now, in the midst of your everyday life.**

God doesn't need you to be perfect to use you; He just needs your activated "Yes." He doesn't need a polished stage; He needs a willing heart. He doesn't need a massive audience; He needs your obedience in your current sphere of influence.

So, how do you fulfill this mission that's already in motion? How do you step into that present call, even when you feel unprepared or small?Here are some concrete, practical ways to activate your mission, starting right where you are:

- **Start with Your Story (Even the "Raggedy" Parts):** You don't need a perfect testimony. Share a small piece of your journey—a moment of breakthrough, a lesson learned, a "next Yes"you took. Use your phone to record a short video, write a brief post, or simply share it in conversation with a trusted friend. Your authenticity is your most powerful credential.

  - *Example*: "I used to hide my past, but God showed me how my business failure was actually preparing me to help others find their true identity in Him. Here's one small step I took..."

- **Serve Your Immediate Sphere:** Your mission field isn't always a faraway land or a grand stage. It's often your family, your workplace, your local community, your church. Look for opportunities to bring hope, encouragement, or practical help right where you are. A kind word, a listening ear, a simple act of service—these are powerful acts of mission.

  - *Example*: "My mission began not with a microphone, but with a simple conversation in the grocery store line, sharing a word of hope with a stranger God put in my path."

- **Leverage What You Already Have:** Don't wait for new equipment, a bigger platform, or more followers. Use the tools in your hand right now. Your smartphone is a powerful recording studio. Social media is a global broadcast station. Your voice is a vessel for truth.

  - *Example*: "I thought I needed a fancy studio to share God's message, but my first impactful video was recorded on my phone, right in my kitchen, sharing a truth God gave me that morning."

- **Focus on "One Person" at a Time:** The Great Commission often feels overwhelming because we think of millions. But Jesus invested deeply in a few. Who is that "one person" in your life, or that "one type" of person you feel called to reach? Focus your energy there.

  - *Example*: "Instead of trying to reach everyone, I started by thinking about that one sister struggling with fear, and I crafted a message just for her. That's where my mission truly began."

- **Embrace Imperfection and Consistency:** The enemy of Activate Your Yes is often perfectionism. Your mission doesn't need to be flawless; it needs to be faithful. Consistent, imperfect effort will always yield more fruit than waiting for the elusive "perfect"moment.

○ *Example:* "My first five-minute devotional wasn't polished, but it was obedient. And that small 'yes' opened the door for countless others."

- **Speak Your Truth in Everyday Interactions:** Your mission isn't limited to formal settings. It lives in your conversations, your responses, and your daily walk. Let your life be a testament to your activated faith.

○ *Example:* "I used to think 'speaking' meant a pulpit, but God showed me my mission was also in the honest conversations with friends, sharing how He brought me through bankruptcy."

Remember, God has already placed His mission within you. It's not about *finding* your mission; it's about **activating the one that's already in motion**. Your obedience, in the small, seemingly insignificant "Yeses" of your everyday life, is the most powerful fuel for the Kingdom of God.

## Chapter 13

# YOU WERE NEVER MEANT TO DO THIS ALONE

**One of the greatest lies the enemy uses to derail your obedience is isolation.** If he can get you to believe that no one else understands what you're going through, you'll shrink back from the very mission you were made to walk in. But hear me, obedience was never meant to be a solo journey.

Jesus sent His disciples two by two. The early church gathered daily, not just for worship, but for encouragement and strengthening. You are not weak because you need people. You are wise. The ones who keep saying Yes aren't the strongest. They're the most surrounded.

You need people who see the vision of your Yes even when you can't. You need people who will pray you back into alignment when your heart starts drifting. You need safe spaces where you can be honest about your resistance, without being shamed for it. Community doesn't just make the Yes possible. It makes it sustainable.

## YOU NEED A "YES" COMMUNITY

Every major moment of obedience in my life has been supported, sometimes carried by the prayers, presence, and encouragement of others. People who didn't just cheer me on when things looked exciting. But people who stayed when the fruit wasn't visible, and the outcome wasn't clear.

God created us for that kind of community. Because He knew we'd need each other to stay faithful. Hebrews 10 says it plainly: "Let us consider how to stir up one another to love and good works... encouraging one another, and all the more as you see the Day drawing near."

> You weren't meant to run this race alone. Your Yes gets stronger when it's lived alongside others who are running faithfully too. You need people you can text when you feel like quitting. You need voices who won't let you shrink back when fear comes in.

You need a small circle, maybe three or four people, who are on the journey with you. These are not perfect people, but present ones—those who show up, pray, and challenge you with love when yourYes starts drifting into silence.

Your obedience was never meant to be private. It was always meant to be part of a body. Jesus didn't send the disciples out one by one.

He paired them.

He planted them.

He prepared them together.

And He's still doing that now.

## WHAT IF YOUR YES UNLOCKS SOMEONE ELSE'S?

Sometimes the most powerful part of your obedience is what it unlocks in someone else. You may never know the full impact of your Yes. But someone is watching. Someone is wondering if it's still worth it. Someone is deciding whether they'll keep going or give up. And your faithfulness, even in the ordinary, even in the invisible, even in the hard, might be the reminder they need that God is still worthy of our trust.

You're not just walking out a calling. You're becoming a living testimony of what it means to say Yes, keep saying Yes, and keep moving—even when it costs you something. That's howKingdom momentum builds. That's how disciples are made. One surrendered, Yes, at a time.

So, will you surrender yours?

# Chapter 14

# ACTIVATION & COMMISSIONING

## YOUR ACTIVATED YES, FOREVER IN MOTION

**This journey of Activate Your Yes is not meant to stay confined within the pages of this book or solely within your quiet time with God.** It's designed to explode into the vibrant, messy, and beautiful reality of your everyday life. God doesn't just want your spiritual Yes; He wants your whole self, including the unique dreams, talents, and passions He has woven into your very being. He delights in using your creativity, your profession, your relationships, and your influence in ways that extend His Kingdom far beyond what you might imagine.

Think of it this way: your Activated Yes isn't just "ministry" in a traditional sense; this is living out your purpose in every sphere.

Here are practical ways your Activated Yes can be fleshed out, demonstrating that God uses your life in all kinds of creative ways:

- **The Creative Catalyst:** If you're an artist, a writer, a musician, a designer, or any kind of creative, your Yes can transform your craft into a vessel for divine truth and beauty.

○ *Practical Example:* You feel a nudge to create. Your Yes means starting that painting, writing that song, designing that website, or crafting that story, even if it's just for an audience of one. It's about infusing your work with the hope, light, or perspective that only comes from God, allowing your art to speak to souls.

- **The Marketplace Minister:** For the entrepreneur, the business owner, the corporate professional, or anyone in the workplace, your "Yes" means operating with integrity, compassion, and excellence that reflects God's character.

○ *Practical Example:* Your Yes is in how you treat your employees, how you serve your customers, how you conduct your negotiations, or how you innovate solutions that genuinely bless people. It's about seeing your desk, your factory floor, or your sales call as a sacred space where God's principles can thrive and impact lives.

- **The Everyday Influencer:** Whether you're a parent, a neighbor, a friend, or a community leader, your Yes activates your influence in your immediate circles.

○ *Practical Example:* Your Yes is in the patient conversation with your child, the genuine compliment to a colleague, the listening ear for a struggling friend, or the courage to speak truth in a local meeting. It's about living out your faith authentically, allowing your life to be a quiet sermon that draws others closer to Christ.

- **The Problem Solver with a Purpose:** If you're passionate about social justice, community development, education, or any area of need, your Yes empowers you to be a solution-bringer.

○ *Practical Example:* Your yes means volunteering at a local shelter, advocating for the marginalized, starting a non-profit, or simply using your voice to highlight an injustice. It's about partnering with God to bring HisKingdom come on earth as it is in heaven, addressing brokenness with divinelove and practical action.

- **The Storyteller of Hope:** Regardless of your profession, your yes activates your ability to share your personal journey and God's faithfulness.

○ *Practical Example:* Your Yes is in sharing a testimony of breakthrough over fear in a casual conversation, posting a vulnerable and encouraging thought on social media, or simply being transparent about your struggles and how God is meeting you in them. It's about letting your life be an open book that points others to the Author of life.

This isn't about adding more to your already full plate; it's about shifting your perspective on what's already *on* your plate. It's about recognizing that every interaction, every project, every relationship is an opportunity for your Activated Yes to shine. God wants to use the very fabric of your life—your personality, your skills, your experiences, and your passions to bring about His purposes.

This is your moment. Not for perfect clarity. Not for a sudden absence of fear. But for unwavering **action**. It's time to follow. To fiercely trust the One who calls. To charge forward, even if your hands are still trembling. To obey—not because it feels easy, but because the God who called you is infinitely worthy.

God never demanded a flawless "Yes." He simply called for a surrendered one. And a surrendered Yes doesn't mean doubt vanishes; it means doubt loses its voice and its power to dictate your next move. So today, right here, before this page turns, let's make an indelible mark. Let's drive a stake deep into the ground.

Believe this truth: Obedience, even in its smallest, most unseen forms, still shatters barriers, transforms lives, and builds the very Kingdom of God. You are not waiting for more resources; you already possess everything you need to ignite this journey. Scripture declares you were custom-made for this purpose. Not for paralysis. Not for hiding. But for powerful, good works that God meticulously prepared for you before you ever drew breath (Ephesians 2:10). So, stride forward, not because the path is smooth, but because His worth demands your every step.

And as you step, remember this profound truth: Your Yes doesn't conclude here. It begins anew—every single morning. Every brutal challenge. Every whisper to quit. Every time you feel overlooked, unsure, or invisible. Your Yes is a living, breathing force that keeps growing. It keeps coming. It relentlessly shapes the unstoppable person God called you to be.

So, as you close this book, know that the true work ofActivate Your Yes is just beginning. It's not a grand, singular event, but a continuous, unfolding journey of small, faithful Yeses that accumulate into a life of profound impact. You are equipped. You are called. You are in motion.

So, take a deep, soul-filling breath. Lift your gaze heavenward. Hold nothing back. And go **Activate Your Yes!**—Spirit-empowered, faith-filled, and with an unshakeable freedom!

Chapter 15

# FINAL SOUL COMMISSION

TODAY, I SAY YES.

SIGNED: ______________________________

DATE:________

WITNESS ( Someone I will allow to hold me accountable):

______________________________

## Want support in activating your yes?

If you're ready to move forward spiritually, emotionally, or strategically, I'd love to support you. Whether you're looking for a speaker, coach, or guide to walk with your church, team, or community...

## Visit www.kimhardy.org

Let's activate what God already put in you.

# ABOUT THE AUTHOR

Kim Hardy is a bestselling author, sought-after keynote speaker, life coach, wife, mother, and grandmother. Kim's unwavering belief is that God is also working and we get to co-labor with Him whenever we activate our yes. She'd love for you to visit with her at www.kimhardy.org.

instagram.com/kimhardyspeaks

facebook.com/kim.w.hardy.5

Made in the USA
Columbia, SC
13 July 2025

60415317R00059